CALIFORNIA
JOURNEYS

Program Consultants
Shervaughnna Anderson · Marty Hougen
Carol Jago · Erik Palmer · Shane Templeton
Sheila Valencia · MaryEllen Vogt
Consulting Author · Irene Fountas

Nature Near and Far 9

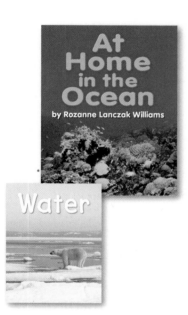

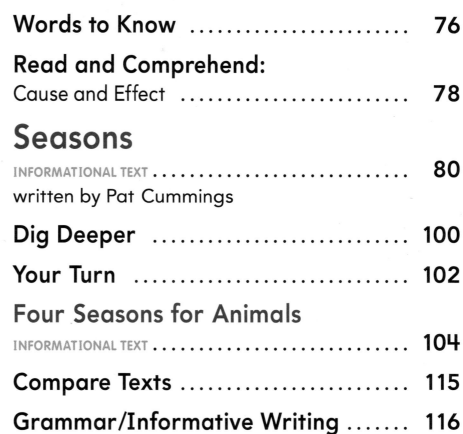

Lesson

15

TOPIC: **Animals**

Be a Reading Detective!

Welcome, Reader!

Your help is needed to find clues in texts. As a **Reading Detective**, you will need to **ask lots of questions.** You will also need to **read carefully.**

▤ myNotebook

As you read, mark up the text. Save your work to **myNotebook.**

- Highlight details.
- Add notes and questions.
- Add new words to **myWordList.**

- Use letters and sounds you know to help you read the words.
- Look at the pictures.
- Think about what is happening.

Let's go!

Nature Near and Far

Stream to Start

> " In all things of nature there is something of the marvelous. "
>
> — Aristotle

Performance Task Preview

At the end of this unit, you will write a report. It will be about reptiles! You will use facts from two texts you read to tell what reptiles are like.

hmhfyi.com

Channel One News®

At
Home
in the
Ocean
by Rozanne Lanczak Williams

Water

🔍 LANGUAGE DETECTIVE

Talk About Words
Work with a partner.
Choose a **Context
Card**. Take out the
yellow word. Put in a
word that means the
same or almost the
same thing. Tell how
the sentences are the
same and different.

≣ myNotebook

Add new words to
myWordList. Use them
in your speaking
and writing.

ELA RF.1.3g, L.1.1j, L.1.5d, L.1.6 ELD ELD.PI.1.6,
ELD.PI.1.8, ELD.PI.1.12b, ELD.PII.1.3a, ELD.PII.1.4

Words to Know

Read Together

▶ Read each **Context Card**.

▶ Make up a new sentence
that uses a blue word.

1 cold
This ocean water is
very cold.

2 where
Sharks live where the
ocean is deep.

3 blue

Today the ocean water looks **blue**.

4 live

Whales **live** in all the oceans of the world.

5 far

Squid swim **far** below the ocean's surface.

6 their

Their home is by the ocean.

7 little

Many **little** fish live in the ocean.

8 water

Some people take photos in the **water**.

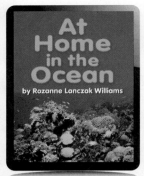

At Home in the Ocean
by Rozanne Lanczak Williams

Read and Comprehend

✓ **TARGET SKILL**

Author's Purpose Authors may write to make you laugh or to give information. The reason an author writes is called the **author's purpose**. In informational texts, the author's purpose is to give information about a topic. As you read, think about what the author wants you to learn. List details that explain the author's purpose.

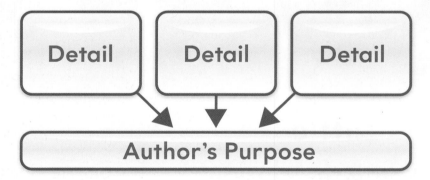

| Detail | Detail | Detail |

Author's Purpose

✓ **TARGET STRATEGY**

Analyze/Evaluate Tell what you think and how you feel about the selection. Tell why.

ELA RI.1.8, RI.1.10a, SL.1.4, SL.1.6, L.1.1j ELD ELD.PI.1.1, ELD.PI.1.3, ELD.PI.1.6, ELD.PI.1.11, ELD.PI.1.12a

Marine Habitats

Oceans are very big. They are filled with many kinds of plants and animals. Some animals live on the bottom of the ocean. Other animals swim far in the water. They come to the top to breathe. Some fish live deep down under the water where it is cold and dark. Some of them can even light up!

You will read more about life in the ocean in **At Home in the Ocean**.

Talk About It

What can you see in the ocean? Write sentences to answer the question. Share your ideas with classmates.

ANCHOR TEXT

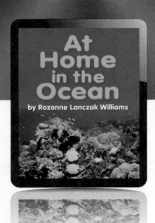

At
Home
in the
Ocean
by Rozanne Lanczak Williams

☑ GENRE

Informational text gives facts about a topic. Look for:
- ▶ information and facts in the words
- ▶ photos that show the real world
- ▶ labels for photos

Meet the Author
Rozanne Lanczak Williams

When Rozanne Lanczak Williams first became a teacher, she lived far from the ocean. She and her students learned a lot about sea life, though, from their research and by making beautiful underwater murals. Now Ms. Williams lives only seven miles from the ocean! To write this story, she hunted for fun fishy facts. She visited a big aquarium, the library, a bookstore, a friend's classroom library—and the ocean!

ELA RI.1.2, RI.1.8, RI.1.10 **ELD** ELD.PI.1.6, ELD.PI.1.7

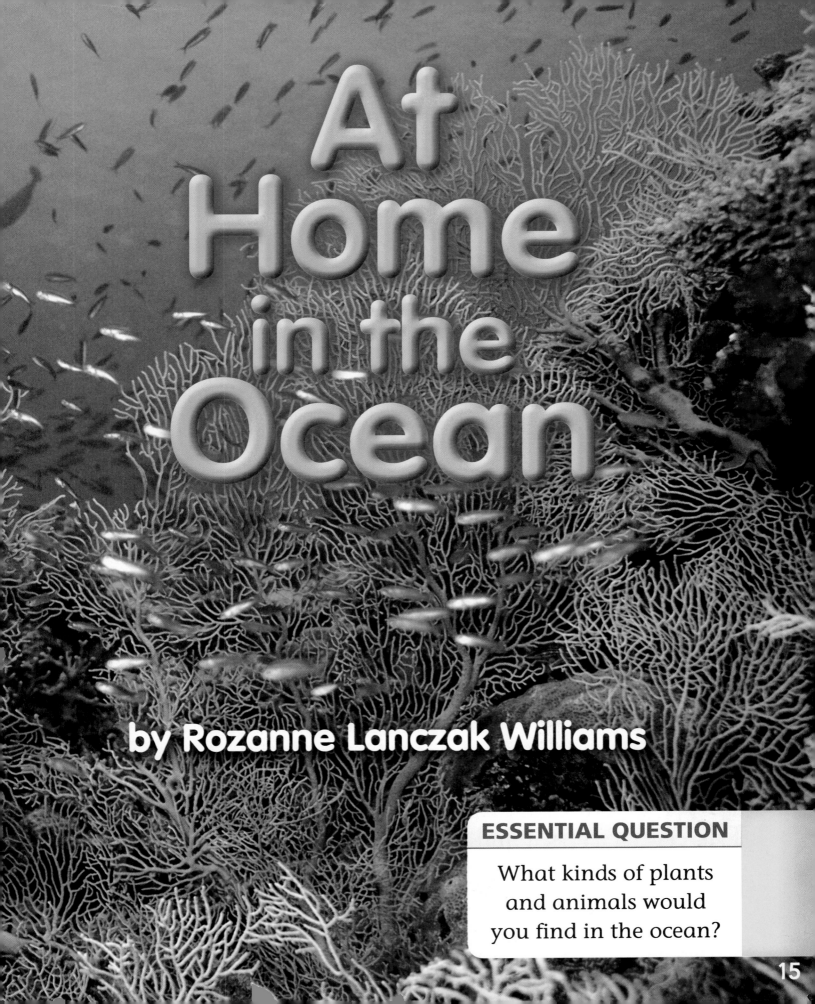

At Home in the Ocean

by Rozanne Lanczak Williams

What kinds of plants and animals would you find in the ocean?

The ocean is big!
It is big and blue as far as you can see.

It is home to many plants and animals.

The biggest animals in the ocean are blue whales. They eat little animals called krill.

blue whale

krill

Many animals live in cold water.
Brrr!

penguins

Penguins swim fast! They flap their wings to zip, zip, zip in the water.

Manatees live where the water is warm.
They do not swim fast.

manatees

Manatees eat lots and lots of plants.
Then they rest.

This turtle swims far!

It digs in the sand and lays its eggs.

Then it swims back to its ocean home.

turtle

eggs

kelp

Kelp is the biggest plant in the ocean.
It can grow fast.

sea otter

Kelp can grow two feet in a day!
Sea otters can get lots of food here.

Lots of plants and animals, big and little, live in the ocean.
The ocean is their home.

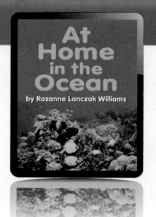

Dig Deeper

Read Together

Use Clues to Analyze the Text

Use these pages to learn about Author's Purpose and Details. Then read **At Home in the Ocean** again.

Author's Purpose

Authors write for many different reasons. Why do you think the author wrote **At Home in the Ocean**? What topic does she want you to learn about? You can find important details in the selection that help explain the author's topic. Use a chart to list the details and the author's purpose.

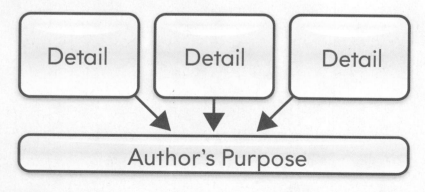

ELA RI.1.2, RI.1.8 ELD ELD.PI.1.6, ELD.PI.1.7

Details

Details are facts and other bits of information. They tell more about a topic. A detail you learned in **At Home in the Ocean** is that manatees eat lots of plants.

What other details from this selection teach you about life in the ocean? You can find important details in the words and pictures.

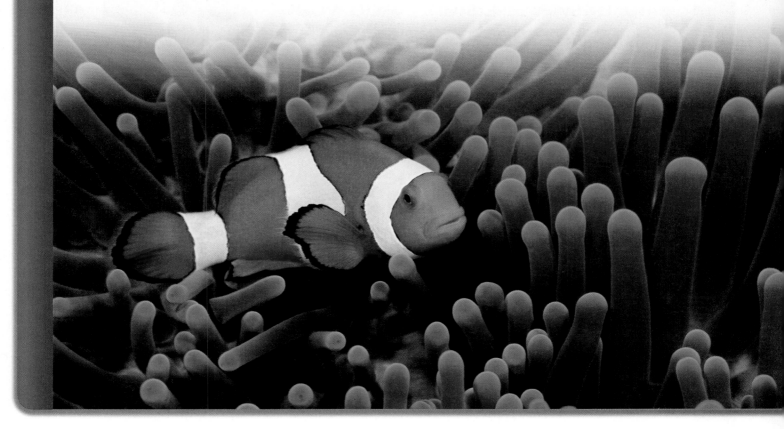

Your Turn

RETURN TO THE ESSENTIAL QUESTION

 **What kinds of plants and animals would you find in the ocean?** Talk with a small group about what you learned. Use details from **At Home in the Ocean** to answer. Listen. Add your ideas to what others say.

 Classroom Conversation

Talk about these questions with your class.

1 Describe an animal or plant you learned about. Use details to tell more.

2 How are all the animals the same?

3 Which animal or plant would you like to learn more about? Why?

ELA RI.1.7, RI.1.8, W.1.2, SL.1.1b, SL.1.4 ELD ELD.PI.1.1, ELD.PI.1.6, ELD.PI.1.7, ELD.PI.1.10, ELD.PI.1.12a, ELD.PI.1.12b

Performance Task

WRITE ABOUT READING ·

Response Write two facts that you learned from **At Home in the Ocean**. Find text evidence in the words and photos to get ideas. Use your own words when you write your facts.

Writing Tip

Add details that give more information about your topic.

Water

Read Together

☑ **GENRE**

Informational text gives facts about a topic. This is from a science textbook.

☑ **TEXT FOCUS**

A **diagram** is a drawing that can show how something works or the parts that make up something. What does the diagram on page 35 show?

Water

What is one thing that all living things, whether they are big or little, have in common? They need water to live.

Water comes in different forms. The water you drink is a liquid. A liquid flows and takes the shape of the container it is in.

ice

water

snow

 Water can freeze into ice or snow.
Frozen water is a solid. A solid has
its own shape.

 What is ice? Ice is water that has
frozen. It is hard and cold.

 Where does snow come from?
Snow is tiny pieces of frozen water
that fall from the clouds.

Ice and snow are found in many places around the world. The North Pole is one of these places. There is cold, blue water all around it. People cannot live that far north for very long, but some animals make their homes near the North Pole.

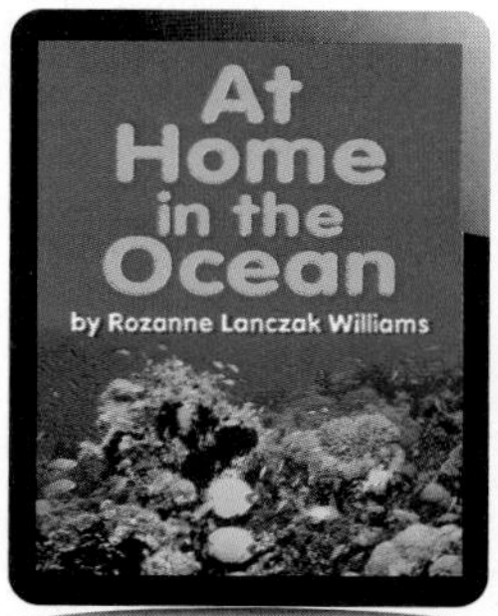

Compare Texts

Read Together

TEXT TO TEXT

Compare Animals Use text evidence to compare the polar bear with an animal from **At Home in the Ocean**. How are they alike and different?

TEXT TO SELF

Describe It Find the photo of your favorite animal from either selection. How does it look? What does it do? Use the photo to help describe it.

TEXT TO WORLD

Use a Globe Use a globe to find two different oceans. Draw and label animals that you think might live in each ocean.

ELA RI.1.3, RI.1.7, RI.1.9, SL.1.4, SL.1.5 ELD ELD.PI.1.6, ELD.PI.1.7, ELD.PI.1.12a, ELD.PI.1.12b

Grammar

Proper Nouns A noun that names a special person, animal, place, or thing is called a **proper noun**. Proper nouns begin with capital letters.

Read Together

Grandstand

Seaside Park

Seal Show

Flip

Shawn Jones

When a **title** is used before a name, it begins with a capital letter, too. A title usually ends with a period.

Mr. Diaz   **Mrs. Sims**   **Miss Reed**

Write each sentence on another sheet of paper. Find the proper nouns. Use capital letters and periods where they belong.

1. My family went to florida.

2. We drove on beach street.

3. We met mrs bell.

4. Her dog is named skippy.

5. I went on the super sun slide.

6. We all ate at snack shack.

Connect Grammar to Writing

When you proofread your writing, be sure you have used capital letters to write proper nouns.

Informative Writing

✓ **Evidence** Sometimes you will write **sentences** that give readers facts. One kind of fact describes how something happens.

Joy wrote about sea lions. Then she added **loudly** to describe how sea lions bark.

Revised Draft

A sea lion can bark. loudly ^

Writing Checklist

✓ **Evidence** Do my sentences have words that tell **how**?

✓ Does my writing tell facts?

✓ Did I use capital letters correctly?

40

ELA W.1.2, W.1.5, L.1.1j **ELD** ELD.PI.1.10, ELD.PI.1.12b, ELD.PII.1.5

Look for words that tell **how** in Joy's final copy. Look for facts. Then revise your writing. Use the Checklist.

Final Copy

Sea Lions

Sea lions do amazing things. A sea lion can bark loudly. It uses its flippers to move quickly on land or in water.

Q **LANGUAGE DETECTIVE**

Talk About Words

Work with a partner. Choose your favorite photo. Tell why it's your favorite. Use as many of the blue words as possible. Be sure to use complete sentences.

Words to Know

Read Together

▶ **Read each Context Card.**

▶ **Describe a picture, using the blue word.**

1 **brown**

Some hyenas have brown fur.

2 **own**

Zebras know their own mother by her stripes.

ELA RF.1.3g, SL.1.6, L.1.1j, L.1.6 ELD ELD.PI.1.3, ELD.PI.1.6, ELD.PI.1.11

3 very

The snake in that tree is very long.

4 off

The bird flew off the rock and into the air.

5 never

Rhinos eat plants. They never eat meat.

6 know

Leopards know how to climb trees.

7 out

I called out to Mom, "Look at that turtle!"

8 been

The giraffes have been moving fast.

How Leopard Got His Spots

Gerald McDermott

Read and Comprehend

☑ **TARGET SKILL**

Sequence of Events Most story events are told in time order. This order is called the **sequence of events.** Good readers think about what happens **first, next,** and **last** so that a story makes sense. You can describe the sequence of events in a flow chart like this.

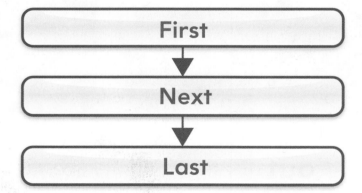

First

↓

Next

↓

Last

☑ **TARGET STRATEGY**

Question Ask yourself questions as you read. Look for text evidence to answer.

ELA RL.1.1, RL.1.3, RL.1.10a, SL.1.4, SL.1.6, L.1.1j ELD ELD.PI.1.1, ELD.PI.1.6, ELD.PI.1.12a, ELD.PII.1.1, ELD.PII.1.2

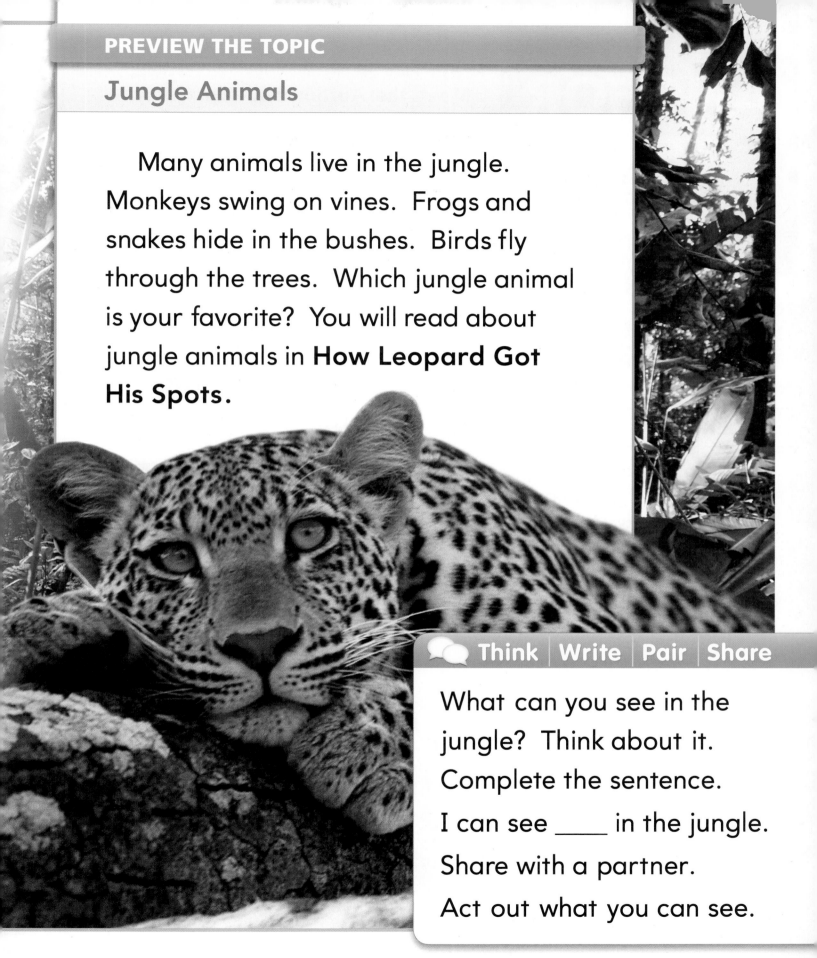

Jungle Animals

Many animals live in the jungle. Monkeys swing on vines. Frogs and snakes hide in the bushes. Birds fly through the trees. Which jungle animal is your favorite? You will read about jungle animals in **How Leopard Got His Spots.**

💬 **Think | Write | Pair | Share**

What can you see in the jungle? Think about it. Complete the sentence.

I can see ____ in the jungle.

Share with a partner.

Act out what you can see.

ANCHOR TEXT

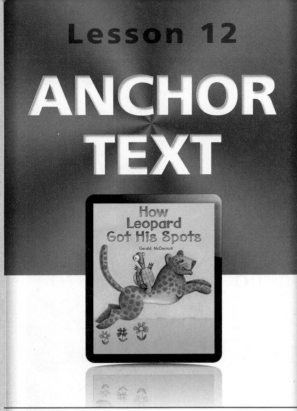

How
Leopard
Got His Spots

Gerald McDermott

✅ GENRE

A **folktale** is an old story people have told for many years. As you read, look for:

▸ a lesson about life

▸ the words **once upon a time**

Meet the Author and Illustrator

Gerald McDermott

When Gerald McDermott was just four years old, he started taking art lessons at a museum. Saturdays were spent at the museum drawing, painting, and looking at the artwork. Mr. McDermott's book **Arrow to the Sun** won the Caldecott Medal for best illustrations.

How Leopard Got His Spots

written and illustrated by Gerald McDermott

47

Do you know how
Leopard got his spots?

Once upon a time, Fred
Turtle was playing catch with
Hal Hyena. Hal tricked Fred.
Then he ran away.

Fred felt very sad.
He called out for help.
"Help! I am stuck in
the plants," he yelled.

Len Leopard ran to help.

Chop! Chop! Chop!
Len cut the plants off and
let Fred out.

Fred and Len danced in the sun.
"This is such fun!" they said.

"I have never been this glad,"
said Fred. "I like to paint if I
am glad!"

Fred mixed paints from many flowers. Then he painted black stripes on Zel Zebra.

Fred painted Jill Giraffe next.
"Look at me!" said Jill.
"I have big brown spots now."

"I like spots very much.
Can I have spots, too?"
asked Len.

Fred got set to paint Len.

58

Now Len had spots
of his very own.

Zel, Jill, and Len had such
fun looking at their spots
and stripes.
Hal said, "Paint me, too!"

But Fred had a trick for Hal.
He splashed Hal with brown
paint. Hal yelled and ran off.

Now Fred and Len
are best friends.

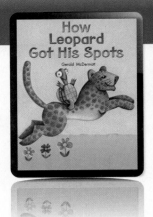

Dig Deeper

Use Clues to Analyze the Text

Use these pages to learn more about Sequence of Events and Story Lesson. Then read **How Leopard Got His Spots** again.

Sequence of Events

In **How Leopard Got His Spots**, Fred Turtle helps Len Leopard get his spots. Think about the important events in the story. What happens **first**, **next**, and **last?** This order is called the **sequence of events**. Use a flow chart like this to describe the order of events in the story.

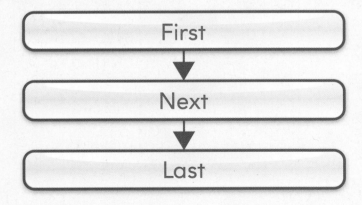

```
┌─────────────────┐
│      First      │
└─────────────────┘
         │
         ▼
┌─────────────────┐
│      Next       │
└─────────────────┘
         │
         ▼
┌─────────────────┐
│      Last       │
└─────────────────┘
```

64

Story Lesson

How Leopard Got His Spots is a folktale. People told this story for many years before it was written down. Folktales often teach a lesson. What lesson do you learn from Hal Hyena?

Folktales can also tell why something is the way it is. Think about Len Leopard's spots. What does this folktale try to explain?

 Read Together

Your Turn

 **Turn and Talk**

How are jungle animals different from animals on a farm? Use the words and pictures in the story to describe the jungle animals. Then draw a jungle animal and a farm animal. Take turns telling how the animals are different.

💬 **Classroom Conversation**

Now talk about these questions with your class.

1 How does Len Leopard help Fred Turtle?

2 Why does Fred splash paint on Hal?

3 What do you think will happen the next time Hal Hyena sees the other animals?

ELA RL.1.1, RL.1.2, RL.1.7, W.1.3, SL.1.1a ELD ELD.PI.1.1, ELD.PI.1.6, ELD.PI.1.10, ELD.PI.1.12a, ELD.PI.1.12b, ELD.PII.1.1, ELD.PII.1.2

WRITE ABOUT READING ····················

Response Write the story the way Hal Hyena would tell it. Write sentences to tell what happens in the beginning, middle, and end of the story.

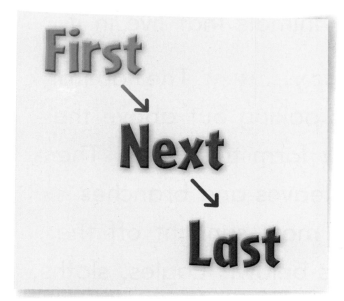

Writing Tip

Add words like **first**, **next**, and **last** to tell the events in order.

INFORMATIONAL TEXT

Read Together

The Rain Forest

A rain forest is a very wet and warm place. Rain forests have layers. Each layer has its own animals that live in it.

Canopy Layer The tops of trees poking out above the forest form this layer. The tree leaves and branches keep most sunlight off the layers below. Eagles, sloths, and monkeys live here.

Understory Layer This layer is above the ground. It is shady. Young trees and bushes grow here. Frogs, birds, and snakes live here.

sloth

eagle

monkey

toucan

jaguar

tapir

69

Forest Floor Not much sunlight reaches this layer. Tapirs, jaguars, and beetles live on the brown forest floor. Ants and giant anteaters also live there. Anteaters have been known to eat thirty thousand insects in a single day!

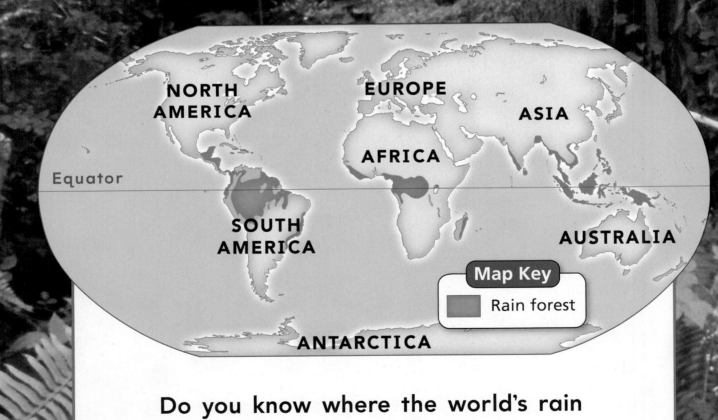

Do you know where the world's rain forests are? This map shows you.

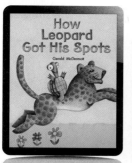

Compare Texts

Read Together

Compare Settings Look at both selections. Tell how the settings are alike and different. Make a chart.

Alike	Different

Write a Story What does **once upon a time** mean? Write a story about an animal you might see near your home. Begin your story with **once upon a time**.

Make a Map Pretend that you are going to visit a rain forest. Draw a map showing where you will go. Explain any symbols or words you use on your map.

ELA RL.1.3, RI.1.3, RI.1.5, W.1.3, L.1.6   ELD ELD.PI.1.6, ELD.PI.1.7, ELD.PI.1.10, ELD.PII.1.1, ELD.PII.1.2

71

Grammar

Commands A sentence that tells someone to do something is a **command**. A command can end with a period. A command can end with an exclamation point when it is said with strong feeling.

Read Together

Commands
Pick up that pencil.
Draw stripes on the zebra.
Help the turtle right now!
Save the rain forest!

Read the sentences. Decide which ones are commands. Write each command on another sheet of paper. Then read the commands to a partner to check them.

1. Paint more spots on the giraffe.

2. Does the leopard like his spots?

3. Stand still while you paint.

4. Those paints are new.

5. Stay away from that wet paint!

Connect Grammar to Writing

When you proofread your writing, be sure you have written commands correctly.

Informative Writing

Read Together

☑ Organization   In good **instructions**, the sentences tell the steps in order. Order words help make the steps easy to follow.

Akil drafted his instructions in a letter to his friend Pam. Later, he added the order word **Last**.

Revised Draft

Last,

4. ~~C~~olor brown spots.
   ^

Writing Checklist

☑ Organization   Do my instructions have order words?

☑ Did I tell the steps in order?

☑ Did I include a greeting and a closing in my letter?

ELA W.1.2, SL.1.2a, L.1.1j **ELD** ELD.PI.1.10, ELD.PII.1.1, ELD.PII.1.2

Revise your writing using the Checklist.
You can follow the instructions in Akil's
final copy to make a puppet!

Final Copy

Dear Pam,

I made a leopard puppet. Here is
how you can make one, too.

1. First, get a small paper bag.
2. Next, fold the sides of the flap.
3. Then, glue on ears, eyes, a nose,
   and whiskers.
4. Last, color brown spots.

I hope you have fun making your
puppet.

Your friend,
Akil

Lesson

13

Seasons
by Pat Cummings

Four Seasons
for Animals

🔍 LANGUAGE DETECTIVE

Talk About Words
Adjectives describe
people, animals,
places, or things by
telling their size,
shape, color, and
number. Work with
a partner. Find the
blue words that are
adjectives. Use them
in complete sentences.

Words to Know

Read
Together

▶ Read each **Context Card**.

▶ **Choose two blue words.**
Use them in sentences.

1 **green**

The green buds come
out in the spring sun.

2 **yellow**

He put on yellow boots
on a rainy day.

ELA RF.1.3g, SL.1.6, L.1.1f, L.1.1j, L.1.6
ELD ELD.PI.1.6, ELD.PII.1.4, ELD.PII.1.5

3 **grow**

Many flowers grow in the summer.

4 **open**

The windows can be open on a hot day.

5 **fall**

The leaves change color in fall.

6 **new**

She has a brand new backpack for school.

7 **down**

Snow comes down on a cold day.

8 **goes**

She goes to the park to skate with her mom.

Read and Comprehend

Read Together

✓ **TARGET SKILL**

Cause and Effect Sometimes one event can **cause** another event to happen. The **cause** happens first. It makes something else happen. The **effect** is what happens next. As you read, think about what happens and why. You can use a chart like this to show how events are connected.

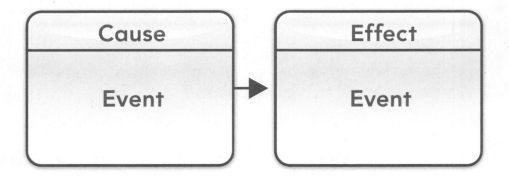

Cause		Effect
Event	→	Event

✓ **TARGET STRATEGY**

Visualize To understand a selection, picture events in your mind as you read.

ELA RI.1.3, RI.1.5, RI.1.10a, SL.1.4, SL.1.6, L.1.1j ELD ELD.PI.1.1, ELD.PI.1.3, ELD.PI.1.6, ELD.PI.1.12a, ELD.PII.1.1, ELD.PII.1.2

Seasons

There are four seasons. In winter it is cold. It snows in some places. Then it gets warmer, and the snow melts. It becomes spring. In spring, plants begin to grow. Summer comes next. It gets hot. Then in fall, the leaves turn colors. It is cool. After fall, it's winter again!

You will read about changes that happen each year in **Seasons**.

🗨 Talk About It

What do you know about the seasons?

What would you like to know?

Share your ideas with your classmates.

What did you learn from others?

ANCHOR TEXT

Seasons
by Pat Cummings

☑ **GENRE**

Informational text gives facts about a topic. As you read, look for:

- ▸ information and facts in the words
- ▸ photos that show the real world

Meet the Author

Pat Cummings

Pat Cummings loves getting letters from kids who have read her books. Sometimes they send her other things too, such as T-shirts, mugs, drawings, and even science projects. **Clean Your Room, Harvey Moon!** is just one of her many books.

ELA RI.1.3, RI.1.4, RI.1.5, RI.1.10 **ELD** ELD.PI.1.3, ELD.PI.1.6, ELD.PI.1.7, ELD.PII.1.1, ELD.PII.1.2

Seasons

written by Pat Cummings

Spring

In the spring,
fresh winds blow.
We plant new seeds,
and green buds grow.

83

Eggs hatch open.

Little chicks sing.

The sun is out.

It must be spring!

The grass gets wet.
Splish! Splash! Splish!
When we step,
we hear it squish.

Summer

Then summer is here
and it gets hot.
We are not in school.
We play a lot.

Bugs buzz and hum.
The plants grow tall.
Next to them,
I look small.

Summer goes fast,
and when it ends,
we will go back to school
with all our friends.

Fall

In fall the leaves
are red, yellow, and brown.
In a gust of wind,
they will fall down.

91

The leaves crunch
as we jump and hop.
It is such fun,
we cannot stop!

Animals get nuts
and pack them away.
They will have lots to eat
on a cold day.

Winter

When it is winter,
cold winds blow.
It is fun to sled
on the soft snow.

When it is cold,
some animals rest.
This animal has
a nap in a nest.

A hat on a shelf
gives us a plan.
We will put the hat
on a big snowman!

Winter

Spring

Summer

Winter, Spring,
Summer, Fall.
Which is best?
We like them all!

Fall

Dig Deeper

Read Together

Use Clues to Analyze the Text

Use these pages to learn about Cause and Effect and Sound Words. Then read **Seasons** again.

Cause and Effect

In **Seasons**, many events cause other events to happen. The **cause** happens first. It is the reason why something else happens. The **effect** is what happens next. In **Seasons**, you read that it is cold in winter. What does the cold cause some animals to do? Use a chart to show what happens and why.

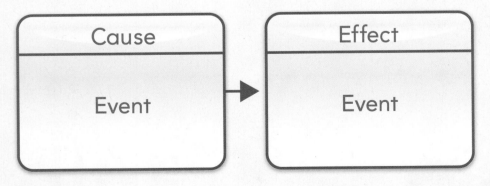

Cause		Effect
Event	→	Event

ELA RI.1.3, RI.1.4, RI.1.5 ELD ELD.PI.1.6, ELD.PI.1.7, ELD.PII.1.1, ELD.PII.1.2

Sound Words

An author can use words that sound like real noises. In the part about spring, the author uses the words **Splish! Splash! Splish!** These words describe the sounds of rain and wet grass.

Find other words that tell about sounds in **Seasons.** Ask yourself what the words mean and what they describe. Use the other words and sentences to help you. Do sound words help you know what real things are like?

Read Together

Your Turn

RETURN TO THE ESSENTIAL QUESTION

Turn and Talk

What changes do the different seasons cause? Talk with a partner about why changes happen in each season. Then look for text evidence to explain your answer. Take turns.

Classroom Conversation

Talk about these questions with your class.

1 What do animals do in different seasons?

2 How do plants change from spring to summer to fall?

3 Tell what the seasons are like where you live.

ELA RI.1.1, RI.1.3, RI.1.5, W.1.1, SL.1.1a ELD ELD.PI.1.1, ELD.PI.1.3, ELD.PI.1.6, ELD.PI.1.10, ELD.PI.1.11, ELD.PI.1.12a, ELD.PII.1.1, ELD.PII.1.2

WRITE ABOUT READING

Response Write about your favorite season. First, tell what your topic is. Then give reasons why you like the season. Use text evidence from **Seasons** for ideas. Write an ending sentence.

Spring

Summer

Fall

Winter

Writing Tip

An ending sentence can tell your opinion again in different words.

INFORMATIONAL TEXT

Read Together

Four Seasons for Animals

✓ GENRE

Informational text gives facts about a topic. Look for facts about what happens to plants and animals during the seasons.

✓ TEXT FOCUS

Headings are titles for different parts of an informational text. They tell you what each section will be about. What do the headings in this selection tell you?

Four Seasons for Animals

written and illustrated
by Ashley Wolff

Spring

It is spring. Young animals run and play. Bird nests are full of eggs. Soon the eggs will hatch.

Spring brings rain. Grass turns green
and grows tall. Buds grow on trees
and plants. Spring also brings rain
puddles! Flower buds get wet. Rain
helps the new plants grow.

Summer

It is summer. Buds open and flowers
bloom in the bright sun. Insects buzz
here and there. Now there are chicks
in the bird nest! Their mother will
teach them how to fly.

It can get very hot in the summer.
Many animals live near the pond.
Ducks swim in the pond. Fox pups
cool off in the shade.

Fall

It is fall. Leaves fall down. Animals get ready for winter. Some animals eat as much as they can. They need to store fat because food is scarce in the winter.

Squirrels and chipmunks gather nuts
so they will have enough food for
the winter.

Winter

It is winter. Winter can be very cold
and wet. Bears hibernate in the winter.
That means they sleep.

Many other animals hibernate in the
winter. They curl up in dens to keep
safe from the cold and wet.

Like all the seasons, the winter will
pass. The animals know that spring
will come once again.

Compare Texts

Read Together

TEXT TO TEXT

Make a Chart How are the selections alike and different? Make a chart to show evidence.

Pictures	Facts	Descriptions

TEXT TO SELF

Describe a Season Describe your favorite season. Tell why you like it. Use details to make your ideas and feelings clear.

TEXT TO WORLD

Tell About Seasons Find your state on a globe. Then locate a country. Tell how you think the seasons in both places might be the same or different.

ELA RI.1.3, RI.1.9, SL.1.4 ELD ELD.PI.1.3, ELD.PI.1.6, ELD.PI.1.9, ELD.PI.1.11, ELD.PI.1.12a, ELD.PI.1.12b

Grammar

Subjects and Verbs In a sentence, the subject and the verb have to agree. Both must tell about the same number of people or things. Add **s** to most **verbs** when they tell about a **noun** that names one.

Read Together

One	More Than One
One **boy** **pull<u>s</u>** his sled.	Two **girls** **pull** their dog.
Brett **slide<u>s</u>** down the hill.	**Children** **slide** across the pond.

Choose the correct verb to finish each sentence. Take turns reading a sentence aloud with a partner. Then talk about how you chose the correct verb.

1. Raindrops _____**?**_____ each spring.
fall   falls

2. Flowers _____**?**_____ in the garden.
grow   grows

3. One bug _____**?**_____ all night.
hum   hums

4. Now the sun _____**?**_____ brightly.
shine   shines

5. The children _____**?**_____ in the pool.
swim   swims

Connect Grammar to Writing

When you proofread your writing, be sure you have written the correct verb to go with each noun.

Informative Writing

✔ **Purpose** When you write **sentences** that tell facts, be sure all your sentences are about one main idea.

Kyle wrote about winter. Then he took out a sentence that didn't belong.

Revised Draft

Winter is the coldest season.

Sometimes it snows here.

~~I have a dog.~~

Writing Checklist

✔ **Purpose** Are all my sentences about one main idea? Do the details tell facts?

✔ Did I write the correct verb to go with each noun?

✔ Did I write a good ending sentence?

ELA W.1.2, W.1.5, L.1.1c ELD ELD.PI.1.10, ELD.PII.1.1

Look for the main idea sentence in Kyle's final copy. Then revise your writing. Use the Checklist.

Final Copy

A Chilly Season

Winter is the coldest season.
Sometimes it snows here.
We go sledding.
The lake freezes.
People skate on it.
Winter is cold, but you can
still go out and play.

Lesson

14

The Big Race
written by Pam Muñoz Ryan
illustrated by Viviana Garofoli

Rules and Laws

🔍 LANGUAGE DETECTIVE

Talk About Words
Work with a partner.
Use two of the blue
words in the same
sentence. Be sure it is
a complete sentence.

Words to Know

Read Together

▶ Read each **Context Card**.

▶ Use a blue word to tell
about something you did.

---

1 **two**

Two desert lizards are
sitting on the rock.

---

2 **into**

The bird flew into the
big cactus.

ELA RF.1.3g, SL.1.6, L.1.1j, L.1.6 ELD ELD.PI.1.6,
ELD.PI.1.12a

3 **three**

There are **three** birds resting in the sun.

4 **starts**

The desert **starts** to cool down at sunset.

5 **over**

A hawk flew **over** the tall rocks.

6 **four**

All **four** legs of this fox are strong.

7 **five**

This desert flower has **five** red spots.

8 **watch**

The rabbits **watch** and listen for danger.

The Big Race

written by Pam Muñoz Ryan
illustrated by Viviana Garofoli

Read and Comprehend

☑ **TARGET SKILL**

Conclusions Sometimes authors do not tell all the details in a story. Readers must use clues in the words and pictures and think about what they already know. This will help them make a smart guess about what the author does not tell. This smart guess is a **conclusion**. Use a chart to list the clues and your conclusions.

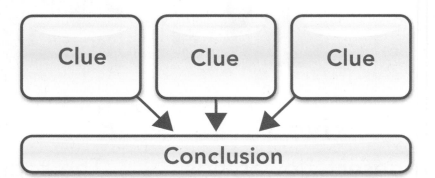

| Clue | Clue | Clue |

Conclusion

☑ **TARGET STRATEGY**

Infer/Predict Use text evidence to help you think of what might happen next.

ELA RL.1.3, RL.1.7, RL.1.10a, RL.1.10b, SL.1.4 ELD ELD.PI.1.1, ELD.PI.1.6, ELD.PI.1.12a

Citizenship

Cross at the crosswalk. This rule keeps you safe. **Wash your hands.** This rule keeps you healthy. Following rules makes you a good classmate. It makes you a good neighbor, too.

When you read **The Big Race,** think about the rules and the different ways the animals race.

 Talk About It

What rules do you follow at school? What rules do you follow at home? Write your answers. Then share your ideas with your classmates.

ANCHOR TEXT

The Big Race

written by Pam Muñoz Ryan
illustrated by Viviana Garofoli

✓ GENRE

A **fantasy** could not happen in real life. As you read, look for:
▸ animals who talk and act like people
▸ events that could not really happen

Meet the Author
Pam Muñoz Ryan

California summers can be very hot. When Pam Muñoz Ryan was growing up, she was often at the library on summer days. That's because the library was one of the few places nearby with air conditioning!

Meet the Illustrator
Viviana Garofoli

Viviana Garofoli and her family make their home in the country of Argentina. **Sophie's Trophy** and **My Big Rig** are two of the books she has illustrated.

The Big Race

written by Pam Muñoz Ryan

illustrated by Viviana Garofoli

Win the Big Race
Win this Big Cake

Today is the big race.

"I like cake!" said Red Lizard.
"I will run in that race."

Red Lizard gets to the race.
Four animals will run with him.

Cottontail is not late.
She will run in lane one.

Rat naps in the shade.

She will run in lane two.

Snake takes his spot in lane three.
Roadrunner stands in lane four.
He waves to his pals.

Red Lizard is in lane five.
The animals bend and hop.

Get set.
Go!

The flag is down, and the race starts!
Many animals watch and clap.

Cottontail does not get far.

Rat falls into the hay.

Snake stops and chases bugs.

Roadrunner trips over a rake.

Who will win?

It's Red Lizard who wins!

"Watch me eat this cake," he yells.
Red Lizard looks at his big cake.

Red Lizard looks at his pals.

His pals like cake, too.
What will Red Lizard do now?

Red Lizard gets five plates.

He gets cake for his pals, too.

Hip, Hip, Hooray for Red Lizard!

Dig Deeper

Use Clues to Analyze the Text

Use these pages to learn about
Conclusions and Cause and Effect.
Then read **The Big Race** again.

Conclusions

You can use clues in **The Big Race** to think about things the author does not say. The author does not tell you why Cottontail does not win. What do the pictures and words show that help you make a smart guess about why? What do you know about races that helps you understand? Use a chart to list clues and conclusions.

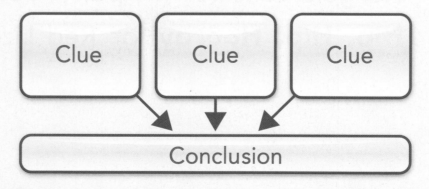

ELA RL.1.3, RL.1.7 ELD ELD.PI.1.6, ELD.PI.1.7

Cause and Effect

Sometimes one event in a story causes another event to happen. As you read, ask yourself what happens and why.

In **The Big Race**, why doesn't Snake win? He does not win because he stops to chase bugs. Snake stopping is the **cause**. What happens after that? Snake loses the race. That is the **effect**.

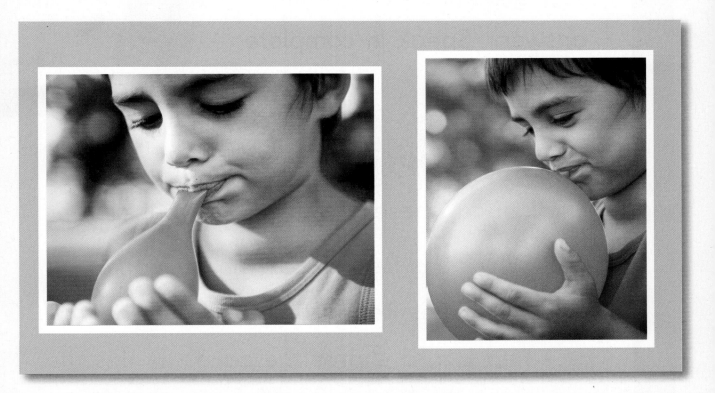

Your Turn

RETURN TO THE ESSENTIAL QUESTION

Turn and Talk

Why is it important to have rules? Describe what happens to the animals in the story when they do not follow the rules. Use text evidence to help you answer. Speak in complete sentences.

 Classroom Conversation

Talk about these questions with your class.

1. Why does Red Lizard win the race?

2. How does Red Lizard feel when he wins?

3. Red Lizard shares the cake. Is this the right thing to do? Why or why not?

ELA RL.1.1, RL.1.7, W.1.1, SL.1.4, SL.1.6 ELD ELD.PI.1.1, ELD.PI.1.3, ELD.PI.1.6, ELD.PI.1.10, ELD.PI.1.11, ELD.PI.1.12a, ELD.PII.1.6

WRITE ABOUT READING ·································

Response Choose a favorite character from **The Big Race**. Write sentences to give reasons why you like him or her. Use details from the story to explain your opinion.

Writing Tip

Use **because** to tell why you think something is true.

INFORMATIONAL TEXT

Read Together

Rules and Laws

Rules and Laws

by J. C. Cunningham

Health Rule

✓ GENRE

Informational text gives facts on a topic. It can be from a textbook, article, or website. Look for facts about rules and laws as you read.

✓ TEXT FOCUS

Labels are words that tell about a picture or photo. They can name a part of a picture or the whole picture. What information do the labels in this selection give?

Rules

   Who needs rules? We all do! Some rules keep us safe and healthy. Some rules help us learn. There are even rules to help us have fun!

Safety Rule

School Rule

Can you find the child following this rule?
Raise your hand to speak. What other rules are the children following? What could happen if they did not follow the rules?

Game Rule

149

Laws

Our government has rules, too. The rules are called laws. Laws keep us safe and healthy. Laws make sure we treat each other fairly.

EMPLOYEES MUST WASH HANDS

Can you find the person who obeyed this law? Employees must wash hands. What other laws do you think the pictures show?

Health Law

Laws help us to be good neighbors and good citizens.

What laws do you think these people are following? How do the laws help?

Who needs
rules and laws?
We all do!

Compare Texts

Read Together

TEXT TO TEXT

Compare Stories Think about the selections. Which is real and which is make-believe? Tell how you know. Take turns sharing evidence with a partner.

TEXT TO SELF

Write a List Write a list of rules the runners should follow in **The Big Race**. Tell why the rules make sense.

TEXT TO WORLD

Map a Race Course Pretend you will run a race through your neighborhood. Where does the race begin? Where is the finish line? Draw a map.

ELA RL.1.5, W.1.2, SL.1.1a, SL.1.1b ELD ELD.PI.1.1, ELD.PI.1.6

Grammar

Verbs and Time Some **verbs** tell what is happening now. Some verbs tell what happened in the past. Add **ed** to most verbs to tell about the past.

Read Together

Now	In the Past
The animals **watch** the race now.	The animals **watch<u>ed</u>** the race yesterday.
They **cheer** for their friends.	They **cheer<u>ed</u>** for their friends.

Try This!

Work with a partner. One partner reads aloud a sentence. The other partner finds the verb. Together, write the verb to tell about the past. Take turns.

1. The runners look at the flag.

2. They start the race.

3. Some racers jump high.

4. They finish the race quickly.

5. The winners pick prizes.

Connect Grammar to Writing

When you proofread your writing, be sure each verb tells clearly if something is happening now or in the past.

Informative Writing

✔ **Evidence** A good **report** needs facts! Before you write, find facts to answer the question you wrote about your topic. Lena found information about lizards. She took notes to remind her of the facts.

Exploring a Topic

Prewriting Checklist

☑ Did I write a good question about my topic?

☑ Will my notes help me remember the facts?

☑ Did I use good sources for information?

Look for facts in Lena's notes. Then record your own notes. Use the Checklist.

Planning Chart

My Question
What do real lizards do?

Fact 1
change color

Fact 2
run fast on back legs

Fact 3
puff up to look big

ELA RF.1.3g, SL.1.2, SL.1.4, SL.1.6, L.1.1b, L.1.1j, L.1.6
ELD ELD.PI.1.6, ELD.PII.1.4, ELD.PII.1.5

🔍 LANGUAGE DETECTIVE

Talk About Words
Nouns are words that name people, animals, things, or places. Work with a partner. Find the blue words that are nouns. Use them in complete sentences. Add details to your sentences to tell more.

Words to Know

Read Together

▶ Read each **Context Card**.

▶ Ask a question that uses one of the blue words.

1 **bird**

An eagle is a bird with big, strong wings.

2 **fly**

Bats are mammals that are able to fly.

160

3 both

The lizard has **both** stripes and spots.

4 long

This kangaroo has a **long** tail.

5 eyes

This dog has blue **eyes**.

6 or

Ducks can either swim **or** fly.

7 those

Those fish are not the same colors.

8 walk

The elephants **walk** together in a group.

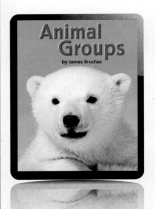

Read and Comprehend

☑ **TARGET SKILL**

Compare and Contrast When you **compare**, tell how things are alike. When you **contrast**, tell how things are different. Think about how things are alike and different to understand a selection better. You can use a diagram to **compare** and **contrast** two things.

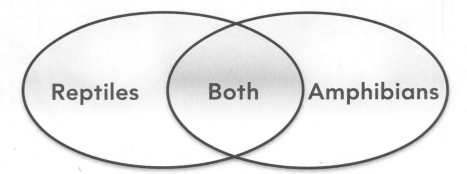

☑ **TARGET STRATEGY**

Monitor/Clarify If a word or a part does not make sense, you can ask questions, reread, or use the pictures for help.

ELA RI.1.3, RI.1.4, RI.1.5, RI.1.10a, SL.1.2, SL.1.3, SL.1.4, SL.1.5 ELD ELD.PI.1.1, ELD.PI.1.6, ELD.PI.1.12a, ELD.PII.1.1

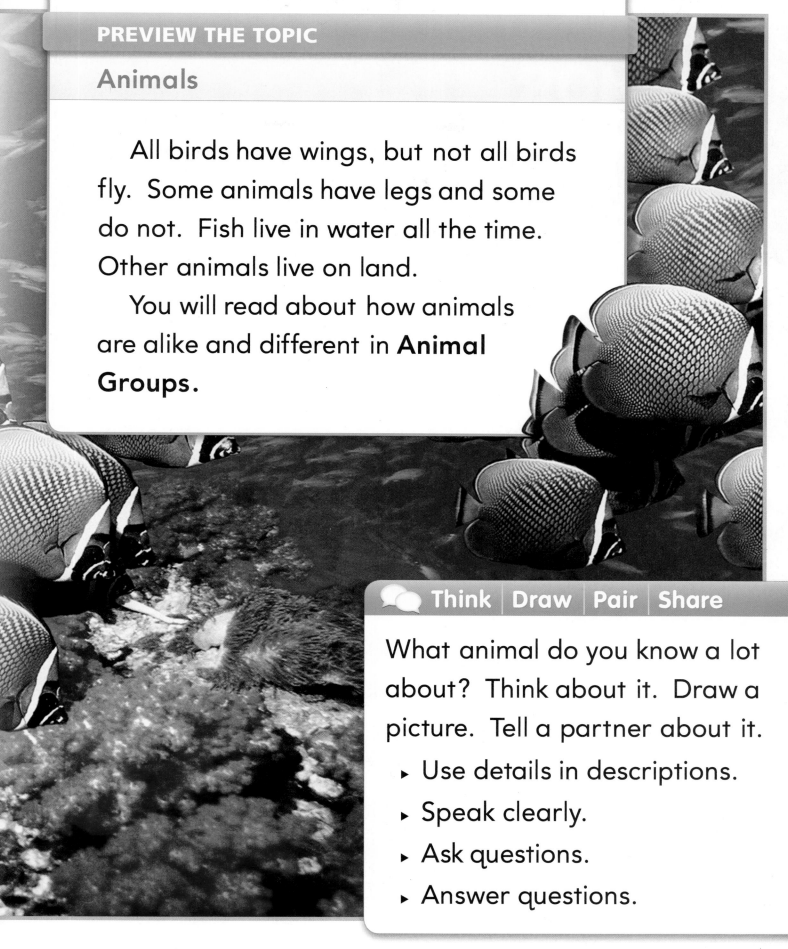

Animals

All birds have wings, but not all birds fly. Some animals have legs and some do not. Fish live in water all the time. Other animals live on land.

You will read about how animals are alike and different in **Animal Groups**.

Think | Draw | Pair | Share

What animal do you know a lot about? Think about it. Draw a picture. Tell a partner about it.

▸ Use details in descriptions.

▸ Speak clearly.

▸ Ask questions.

▸ Answer questions.

ANCHOR TEXT

Animal Groups
by James Bruchac

Informational text
gives facts about a
topic. As you read,
look for:
▶ information and
  facts in the words
▶ photos that show
  the real world

Meet the Author
James Bruchac

James Bruchac has many
interests. He is a writer, a
storyteller, an animal tracker,
and a wilderness guide.
Together with his father, Joseph
Bruchac, he wrote the books
How Chipmunk Got His Stripes
and **Turtle's Race with Beaver**.

Animal Groups

written by James Bruchac

ESSENTIAL QUESTION

What makes birds
different from
mammals?

165

Fish

Reptile

Amphibian

Let's take a look at five animal groups.

Bird

Mammal

How are animals in a group the same?

Fish

fin

eye

mouth

gill

fin

Fish must live in water. Fish have gills that help them breathe in water.

tail

Fish have fins and tails. Those help them swim.

Fish can be many shapes and sizes.
Can you find a fish in this picture?

Reptiles

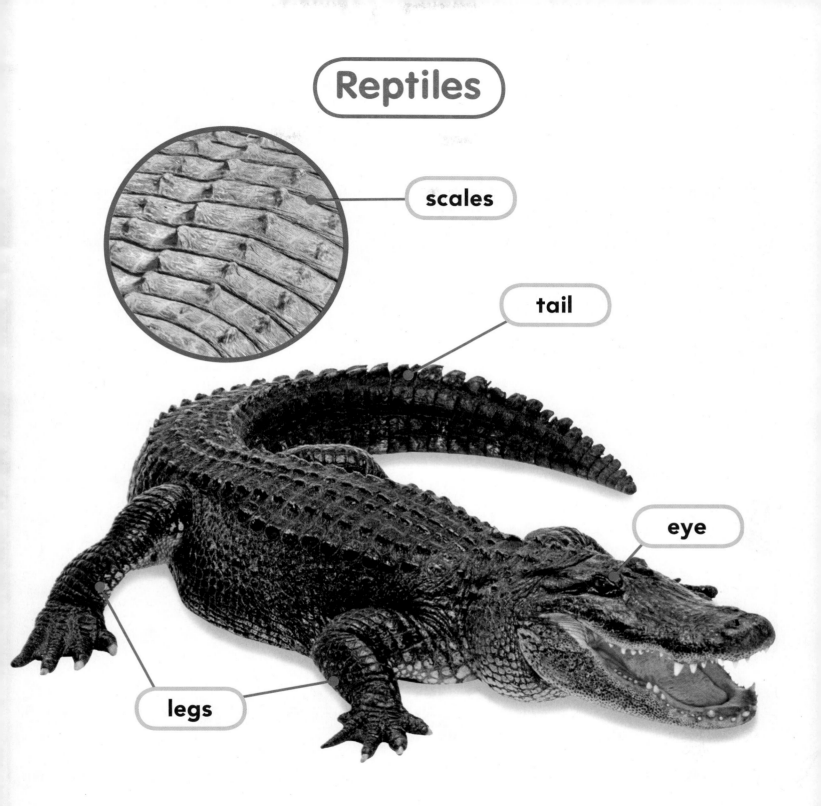

scales

tail

eye

legs

Reptiles can live on land. Some like to be in water. Reptiles have scales on their skin.

Many reptiles hatch from eggs.

Snakes cannot walk. They do not have legs. This snake slides its long body on the grass.

Amphibians

eye

wet skin

legs

Amphibians spend time both on land
and in water. They do not have scales.
Their skin is wet.

tadpoles

Amphibians hatch from eggs.
Tadpoles hatch and grow to be frogs.

Birds

eye

bill

wing

feathers

A bird has feathers and wings. This
bird's eyes are on the sides of its face!

Many birds can fly. Some can run
or swim fast.

Birds hatch from eggs. This hen made a nest for its eggs.

Mammals

eye

hair

tail

legs

Mammals can be many shapes and sizes.
They have hair on their skin.

A mammal mom can
make milk for its baby.

Lots of mammals live on land,
but some live in water.

Did you know that you
are a mammal, too?

Dig Deeper

Read Together

Use Clues to Analyze the Text

Use these pages to learn about Compare and Contrast and Text and Graphic Features. Then read **Animal Groups** again.

Compare and Contrast

In **Animal Groups,** you learned what makes animals in a group the same and different. Think about reptiles and amphibians. **Compare** the groups to tell how they are alike. **Contrast** the groups to tell how they are different. Use a diagram to compare and contrast groups.

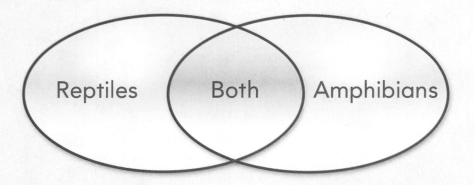

Reptiles · Both · Amphibians

 ELA RI.1.3, RI.1.5, RI.1.7 ELD ELD.PI.1.6, ELD.PII.1.1

Text and Graphic Features

Authors use special features to point out information. **Headings** are often at the top of a page and tell what part you are reading. **Labels** are words that give more information about details in pictures.

The heading on page 168 is **Fish**. What is this part about? There are also labels that give information. What do you learn about a fish's body?

Your Turn

RETURN TO THE ESSENTIAL QUESTION

Turn and Talk

What makes birds different from mammals? Choose an animal from each group. Use words and pictures from the selection to tell how the animals are alike and different. Ask questions if you do not understand your partner's ideas.

Classroom Conversation

Talk about these questions with your class.

1 How are all mammals alike?

2 How are fish different from mammals?

3 What are the five animal groups? What new things did you learn?

ELA RI.1.3, RI.1.5, RI.1.7, W.1.8, SL.1.1c, SL.1.3 ELD ELD.PI.1.1, ELD.PI.1.5, ELD.PI.1.6, ELD.PI.1.10, ELD.PI.1.12a, ELD.PII.1.1

WRITE ABOUT READING ....

Response Use facts you learned from the selection to write a riddle about an animal. Write clues. Do not give its name. Read your riddle to a partner. Have your partner use the evidence in the clues to guess the answer.

I have gills and live in water.

Writing Tip

Use a question mark (**?**) at the end of a question.

PLAY

Read Together

Animal Picnic

☑ GENRE

A **play** is a story that people act out. Most of the words in a play are the words the characters say.

☑ TEXT FOCUS

Stage directions are extra words in a play that tell about the characters and setting. They also tell what actions characters do. What are the stage directions in this play? How do you know?

Animal Picnic

by Debbie O'Brien

Cast of Characters

 Fox

 Cow

 Bird

 Hi, Cow and Bird. How was your trip?

 I had to walk to get here.

 I had to fly.

(pointing to Cow's basket)
What food did you bring for
our picnic?

I brought grass. I use my flat
teeth to grind it.

I brought meat. I use my long,
sharp teeth to eat it.

We both have teeth, but we
eat different things!

(pointing to Bird's basket)
What did you bring,
Bird?

189

I did not bring grass or meat. I brought seeds. Birds don't have any teeth!

How will you eat those seeds without teeth?

Watch this!
(Bird eats some seeds.)
Yum, yum, yum!

190

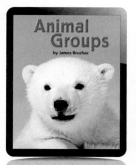

Compare Texts

Read Together

TEXT TO TEXT

Compare Information Think about both selections. How are they alike and different? What information do you learn in each selection?

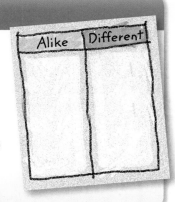

TEXT TO SELF

Talk About Animals Which animal group is your favorite? Talk about it with a partner. Use complete sentences.

TEXT TO WORLD

Write a Question Write a question you have about an animal in the selections. Use this book or other books to find the answer.

ELA RI.1.1, RI.1.9, W.1.8, SL.1.6 ELD ELD.PI.1.1, ELD.PI.1.3, ELD.PI.1.6, ELD.PI.1.11, ELD.PI.1.12a

Grammar

Read
Together

The Verb be The verbs **is** and **are** tell what is happening now. Use **is** with a noun that names one.

One	More Than One
This **chick** **is** small.	Two **chicks** **are** small.

The verbs **was** and **were** tell what happened in the past. Use **was** with a noun that names one.

One	More Than One
One **egg** **was** here.	Two **eggs** **were** here.

Read each sentence aloud two times, saying a different verb each time. Ask your partner to repeat the sentence with the correct verb. Then switch roles.

1. Animals _____?_____ many sizes.
            is   are

2. This frog _____?_____ small.
            is   are

3. A frog _____?_____ once a tiny tadpole.
           was   were

4. Lions _____?_____ little cubs.
           was   were

5. The snake _____?_____ long and thin.
           is   are

Connect Grammar to Writing

When you proofread your writing, be sure you have used the verbs **is**, **are**, **was**, and **were** correctly.

Informative Writing

☑ **Elaboration** In a good **report**, the right words make the facts easy to understand. Lena drafted her report. Later, she wrote different words to make her meaning clear.

Revised Draft

Some lizards puff up ^to
with air
bigger to an enemy.
look big. ^

Revising Checklist

☑ Did I use words that make my meaning clear?

☑ Did I use correct punctuation?

☑ Did I spell words correctly?

☑ Did I write a good ending sentence?

ELA W.1.2, W.1.5, L.1.2b, L.1.2d ELD ELD.PI.1.10, ELD.PI.1.12b, ELD.PII.1.5

Look for exact words in Lena's final copy. Then revise your writing. Use the Checklist.

Final Copy

An Interesting Reptile

Lizards do some funny things. Some can change color quickly. Others run fast using only their back legs. Some lizards puff up with air to look bigger to an enemy. Lizards are very interesting reptiles.

Write a Report

TASK Look at **At Home in the Ocean** and **Animal Groups.** Think about the different kinds of animals. Then write a report to explain to a friend or family member what reptiles are like.

PLAN ·· myNotebook

Use the tools in your eBook to remember facts about reptiles.

Gather Information Talk with a group about the reptiles in **Animal Groups** and the turtles in **At Home in the Ocean.** What did you learn about reptiles?

Write facts about reptiles on a chart.

- What will your report be about? This is the topic.

- How are all reptiles alike?

- Name and describe some reptiles. Tell how they move.

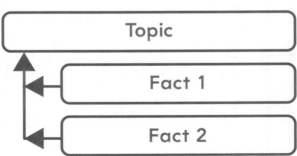

Write your draft in *my*WriteSmart.

Write Your Report   Follow these steps.

Topic Sentence

Write a topic sentence to tell the main idea of your report. Here are sentence ideas.

Reptiles are interesting because _____.

You can tell an animal is a reptile because _____.

Facts

Write sentences that tell facts about reptiles. Use your chart for ideas. Use the right verbs to go with the nouns. Add details to make your meaning clear.

All reptiles _____.

A _____ is an interesting reptile.

It has _____, _____, and _____.

It uses its _____ _____ to _____.

Ending

Write an ending for your report. Use one of these ideas or your own idea.

- Retell the main idea in different words.
- Tell the most interesting thing about reptiles.

197

my WriteSmart

Review Your Draft Read your writing and make it better. Use the Checklist.

Ask a partner to read your draft. Talk about how you can make it better.

☑ Did I explain what a reptile is?

☑ Does my topic sentence tell the main idea of my report?

☑ Did I use information from the texts to write my facts? Do I have examples of reptiles?

☑ Does each sentence have the correct verb?

☑ Did I spell words correctly?

PRESENT

Share Make a final copy of the report. Add pictures. Pick a way to share.

- Pretend you are on TV. Read your report.

- Glue your report to a reptile shape.

Amazing Reptiles

Words to Know

Unit 3 High-Frequency Words

⑪ At Home in the Ocean

blue	where
far	water
live	cold
little	their

⑫ How Leopard Got His Spots

brown	never
own	know
very	out
off	been

⑬ Seasons

green	fall
yellow	new
grow	down
open	goes

⑭ The Big Race

two	over
into	four
three	five
starts	watch

⑮ Animal Groups

bird	eyes
fly	or
both	those
long	walk

Glossary

A

amphibians
An **amphibian** is an animal that
lives in water and on land.
Frogs are **amphibians**.

B

biggest
Something that is the **biggest** is bigger in size than
anything else. The whale is the **biggest** animal in
the ocean.

blow
To **blow** means to push air. The winds **blow** the cold air
across the land.

body
The **body** of a person or animal is made up of the parts
you can see and touch. We are learning about the parts
of the **body**.

breathe

To **breathe** is to take in breaths of air. I **breathe** in the fresh air when I am outside.

C

cottontail

A **cottontail** is a kind of rabbit. That **cottontail** has a white fluffy tail.

D

danced

To **dance** means to move to music. We played music and **danced** for hours.

day

A **day** is the time from one morning to the next morning. Tuesday was a sunny **day**.

F

feathers

A **feather** is a part of a bird. The bird had soft **feathers**.

feet

A foot is a measurement that equals 12 inches. **Feet** means more than one foot. Some trees can grow as tall as 100 **feet**.

flowers

A **flower** is a part of a plant. We planted pretty **flowers** in the garden.

G

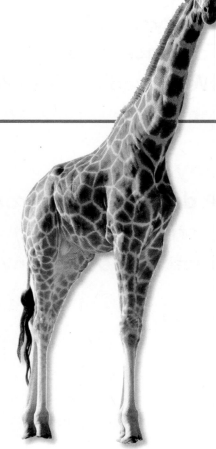

giraffe

A **giraffe** is a tall spotted animal with a long neck. The **giraffe** ate leaves from the top of the tree.

group

A **group** is a number of people or things together. A **group** of us went swimming last Saturday.

grow

When plants and animals **grow**, they get bigger and bigger. Kittens **grow** and become cats.

H

hair

Hair is what grows on your head. My dad cuts my **hair** when it gets too long.

hay

Hay is a kind of grass that has been cut and dried. My horse likes to eat **hay**.

home

A **home** is a place where people or animals live. Jellyfish make their **home** underwater.

hooray

Hooray is something people shout when they are happy. When I hit a home run, my parents yelled **hooray!**

hyena

A **hyena** is a wild animal that looks like a dog. The **hyena** is found in Africa and Asia.

L

leaves

A **leaf** is a part of a plant. In the fall, the **leaves** turn pretty colors.

leopard

A **leopard** is a wild animal that looks like a cat with spots. The **leopard** paced in its cage.

lions

A **lion** is a large wild animal that looks like a big cat. We saw a movie about **lions** in Africa.

lizard

A **lizard** is a small reptile. The **lizard** lay on the rock in the hot sun.

M

mammals

A **mammal** is a warm-blooded animal. Cats are **mammals**.

manatees

A **manatee** is a plant-eating animal with flippers and a flat tail that lives in warm water. When we visited Florida, we saw **manatees** swimming in the water.

O

ocean

An **ocean** is a large body of salt water. It's fun to sail on the **ocean**.

P

paint

To **paint** means to cover something with color. Aunt Carly likes to **paint** houses.

penguins

A **penguin** is a kind of bird that lives in cold places. **Penguins** keep their chicks warm.

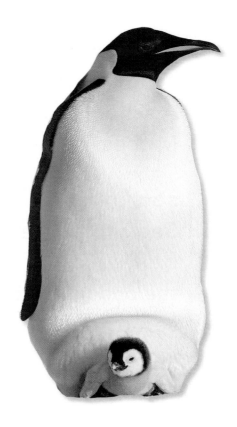

R

race

A **race** is a contest to find out who is the fastest. Selena got to the finish line first and won the **race**.

reptiles

A **reptile** is a cold-blooded animal. Snakes are **reptiles.**

roadrunner

A **roadrunner** is a very fast bird. We saw a **roadrunner** in the Arizona desert.

S

school

A **school** is a place where students learn from teachers. My best friend and I go to the same **school**.

sea otters

Sea otters are mammals with thick, brown fur that live in and by the ocean. After a swim, **sea otters** like to sit in the warm sun.

seeds

A **seed** is a part of a plant. Most plants grow from tiny little **seeds**.

snow

Snow is tiny pieces of frozen water that fall from the clouds. When we woke up, the ground was covered with **snow**.

snowman

A **snowman** looks like a person made of snow. We piled three balls of snow on top of each other and made a **snowman**.

spring

Spring is the season that comes after winter. In the **spring**, the flowers begin to bloom.

summer

Summer is the season that comes after spring. This **summer** my family will go to the beach.

T

tadpoles

A **tadpole** is a baby frog. I found **tadpoles** swimming in our pond.

tails

A **tail** is a part of some animals' bodies. Rats have long **tails**.

tall

To be **tall** is to stand high above the ground. The giraffe is very **tall**.

turtle

A **turtle** is a reptile with a shell. The **turtle** went inside its shell as soon as I touched it.

W

warm

Warm means not very hot. The tea was still **warm** after it sat for a while.

whales

A **whale** is the biggest mammal that lives in the ocean. When we went boating, we saw **whales** as big as our boat!

wings

A **wing** is a part that helps something to fly. The bird flapped its **wings** and flew away.

winter

Winter is a season that comes after fall. Last **winter** was very cold!

Z

zebra

A **zebra** is a striped animal that looks like a horse. My favorite animal is the **zebra**.

Credits